Zion Lutheran Church.

GOD'S
Little Helper

written by Toby Graff

illustrated by Gwen Connelly

Library of Congress Catalog Card No. 86-63567
©1987. The STANDARD PUBLISHING Company, Cincinnati, Ohio
Division of STANDEX INTERNATIONAL Corporation. Printed in U.S.A.

God has so many things to do.
Could He use a helper like me?
I'd like to help Him any way I can,
and I'd even work for free.

But how would I know just what to do
to make the world run right?
I'd need to know about everything
from peanuts to anthracite.

How would I ever figure out
   what every animal should eat?
Some eat only vegetables
   and others only meat.

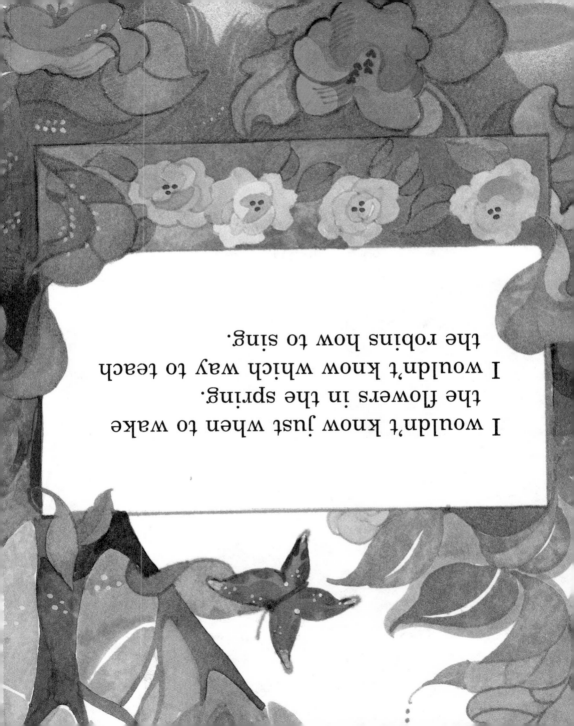

I wouldn't know just when to wake
the flowers in the spring.
I wouldn't know which way to teach
the robins how to sing.

I don't know how to build a nest.
How could I teach the birds?
Besides, I don't know their language,
for they don't use human words.

How could I place a whole new life
    into a tiny seed?
How would I know
    there's a flower inside
and not a baby weed?

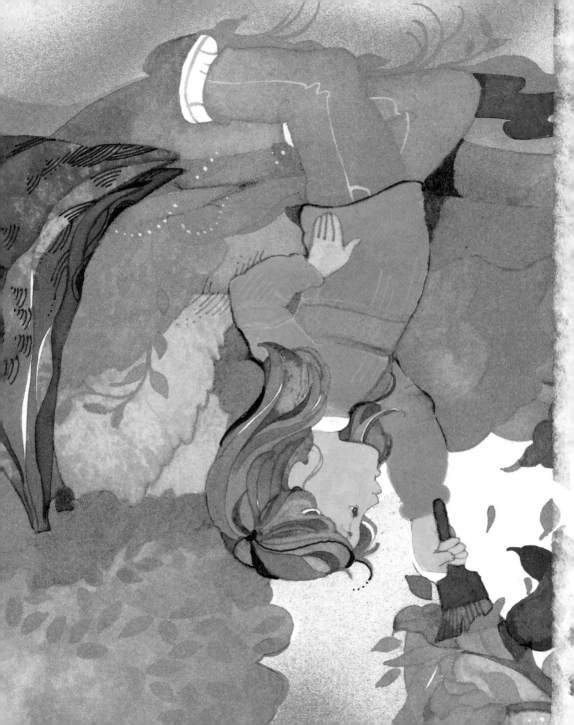

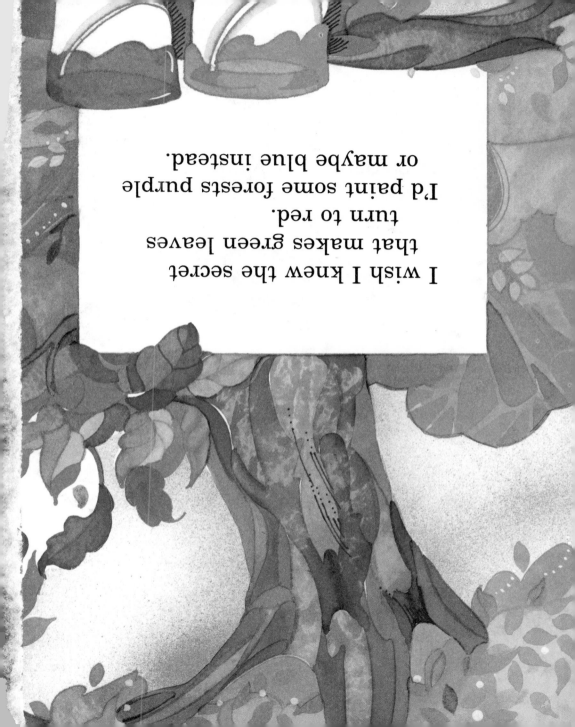

I wish I knew the secret
that makes green leaves
turn to red.
I'd paint some forests purple
or maybe blue instead.

I'd have to be friendly with crocodiles
and snakes and lizards too.
I think it would be much easier
to be friends with kangaroos.

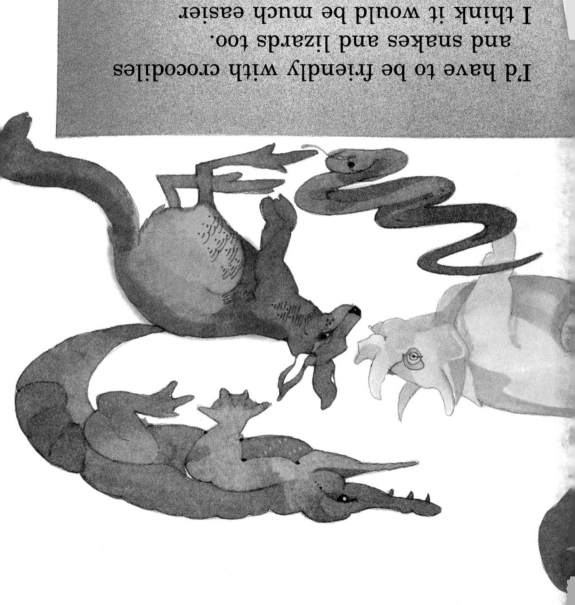

How would I keep the sun just right
  for people to feel warm?
And how would I know when the time
    is right
    send a big thunderstorm?

How could I ever hope to feed
all the monkeys by myself?
I'd have to keep ten bunches
of bananas on my shelf!

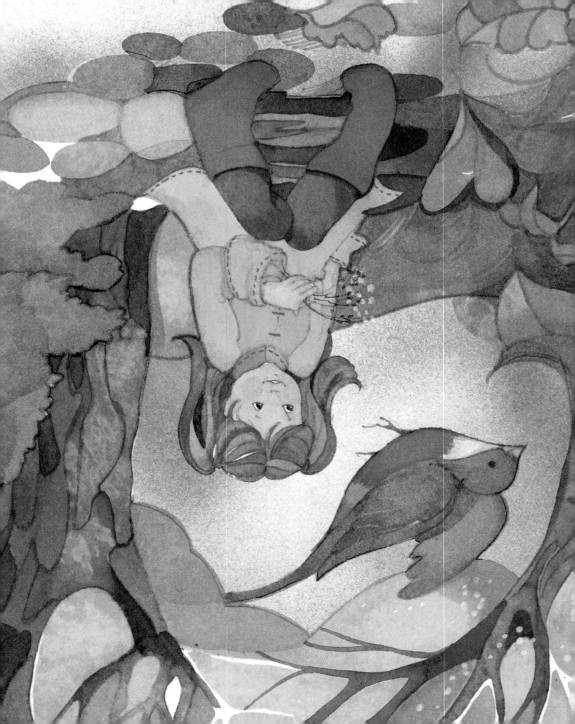

How could I teach a bird to fly
   when I have no wings of my own?
I couldn't get more than a foot off the
     ground,
   even with a grunt and a groan.

I just don't know the best way to hold
the stars up in the sky.
How could I even reach them?
They're all so very high.

And how could I ever give enough love
to every person in the world?
All those hugs, one after the other,
would put me in a swirl.

Maybe I'll leave that up to God.
  The job's too big for me.
But I'm sure there's work that I can do
  from now to eternity.

I think I'll start by watering
all the flowers in our yard.
And maybe I'll give my brother a hug.
That wouldn't be too hard.

I'm sure that God is happy
with the things I do each day.
For He loves me when I'm working,
and He loves me when I play.